MW00901400

Your purchase of the Accounting Ledger and Bill Planner Book is greatly appreciated. We are working hard to build even better books for you. We would greatly appreciate if you would provide a review and comments on Amazon.com.

Thank you!

This Accounting Ledger belongs to:

Sheet Number ____________________

INCOME & EXPENSES				BALANCE
DATE	TRANSACTION DETAILS	Expense Debit (-)	Income Credit (+)	

Sheet Number ________________

INCOME & EXPENSES				BALANCE
DATE	TRANSACTION DETAILS	Expense Debit (-)	Income Credit (+)	

Sheet Number ________________

INCOME & EXPENSES				BALANCE
DATE	TRANSACTION DETAILS	Expense Debit (-)	Income Credit (+)	

Sheet Number ________________

INCOME & EXPENSES				BALANCE
DATE	TRANSACTION DETAILS	Expense Debit (-)	Income Credit (+)	

Sheet Number ____________

INCOME & EXPENSES				BALANCE
DATE	TRANSACTION DETAILS	Expense Debit (-)	Income Credit (+)	

Sheet Number ________________

INCOME & EXPENSES				BALANCE
DATE	TRANSACTION DETAILS	Expense Debit (-)	Income Credit (+)	

Sheet Number ___________________

INCOME & EXPENSES				BALANCE
DATE	TRANSACTION DETAILS	Expense Debit (-)	Income Credit (+)	

Sheet Number ________________

INCOME & EXPENSES				BALANCE
DATE	TRANSACTION DETAILS	Expense Debit (-)	Income Credit (+)	

Sheet Number ____________________

INCOME & EXPENSES				BALANCE
DATE	TRANSACTION DETAILS	Expense Debit (-)	Income Credit (+)	

Sheet Number ________________

INCOME & EXPENSES				BALANCE
DATE	TRANSACTION DETAILS	Expense Debit (-)	Income Credit (+)	

Sheet Number ________________

INCOME & EXPENSES				BALANCE
DATE	TRANSACTION DETAILS	<u>Expense</u> Debit (-)	<u>Income</u> Credit (+)	

Sheet Number ________________

INCOME & EXPENSES				BALANCE
DATE	TRANSACTION DETAILS	Expense Debit (-)	Income Credit (+)	

Sheet Number ________________

INCOME & EXPENSES				BALANCE
DATE	TRANSACTION DETAILS	Expense Debit (-)	Income Credit (+)	

Sheet Number ________________

INCOME & EXPENSES				BALANCE
DATE	TRANSACTION DETAILS	Expense Debit (-)	Income Credit (+)	

Sheet Number ________________

INCOME & EXPENSES				BALANCE
DATE	TRANSACTION DETAILS	Expense Debit (-)	Income Credit (+)	

Sheet Number ____________________

INCOME & EXPENSES				BALANCE
DATE	TRANSACTION DETAILS	Expense Debit (-)	Income Credit (+)	

Sheet Number ________________

INCOME & EXPENSES				BALANCE
DATE	TRANSACTION DETAILS	Expense Debit (-)	Income Credit (+)	

Sheet Number ________________

INCOME & EXPENSES				BALANCE
DATE	TRANSACTION DETAILS	Expense Debit (-)	Income Credit (+)	

Sheet Number ________________

INCOME & EXPENSES				BALANCE
DATE	TRANSACTION DETAILS	Expense Debit (-)	Income Credit (+)	

Sheet Number ________________

INCOME & EXPENSES				BALANCE
DATE	TRANSACTION DETAILS	Expense Debit (-)	Income Credit (+)	

Sheet Number ________________

INCOME & EXPENSES				BALANCE
DATE	TRANSACTION DETAILS	Expense Debit (-)	Income Credit (+)	

Sheet Number ________________

INCOME & EXPENSES				BALANCE
DATE	TRANSACTION DETAILS	Expense Debit (-)	Income Credit (+)	

Sheet Number ________________

INCOME & EXPENSES				BALANCE
DATE	TRANSACTION DETAILS	Expense Debit (-)	Income Credit (+)	

Sheet Number ________________

INCOME & EXPENSES				BALANCE
DATE	TRANSACTION DETAILS	Expense Debit (-)	Income Credit (+)	

Sheet Number ________________

INCOME & EXPENSES				BALANCE
DATE	TRANSACTION DETAILS	Expense Debit (-)	Income Credit (+)	

Sheet Number ________________

INCOME & EXPENSES				BALANCE
DATE	TRANSACTION DETAILS	Expense Debit (-)	Income Credit (+)	

Sheet Number _______________

INCOME & EXPENSES				BALANCE
DATE	TRANSACTION DETAILS	Expense Debit (-)	Income Credit (+)	

Sheet Number ________________

INCOME & EXPENSES				BALANCE
DATE	TRANSACTION DETAILS	Expense Debit (-)	Income Credit (+)	

Sheet Number ________________

INCOME & EXPENSES				BALANCE
DATE	TRANSACTION DETAILS	Expense Debit (-)	Income Credit (+)	

Sheet Number ________________

INCOME & EXPENSES				BALANCE
DATE	TRANSACTION DETAILS	Expense Debit (-)	Income Credit (+)	

Sheet Number ________________

INCOME & EXPENSES				BALANCE
DATE	TRANSACTION DETAILS	Expense Debit (-)	Income Credit (+)	

Sheet Number ________________

INCOME & EXPENSES				BALANCE
DATE	TRANSACTION DETAILS	Expense Debit (-)	Income Credit (+)	

Sheet Number ________________

INCOME & EXPENSES				BALANCE
DATE	TRANSACTION DETAILS	Expense Debit (-)	Income Credit (+)	

Sheet Number ________________

INCOME & EXPENSES				BALANCE
DATE	TRANSACTION DETAILS	Expense Debit (-)	Income Credit (+)	

Sheet Number ________________

INCOME & EXPENSES				BALANCE
DATE	TRANSACTION DETAILS	Expense Debit (-)	Income Credit (+)	

Sheet Number ________________

INCOME & EXPENSES				BALANCE
DATE	TRANSACTION DETAILS	Expense Debit (-)	Income Credit (+)	

Sheet Number ______________

INCOME & EXPENSES				BALANCE
DATE	TRANSACTION DETAILS	<u>Expense</u> Debit (-)	<u>Income</u> Credit (+)	

Sheet Number ________________

INCOME & EXPENSES				BALANCE
DATE	TRANSACTION DETAILS	Expense Debit (-)	Income Credit (+)	

Sheet Number ________________

INCOME & EXPENSES				BALANCE
DATE	TRANSACTION DETAILS	Expense Debit (-)	Income Credit (+)	

Sheet Number ________________

INCOME & EXPENSES				BALANCE
DATE	TRANSACTION DETAILS	<u>Expense</u> Debit (-)	<u>Income</u> Credit (+)	

Sheet Number ______________

INCOME & EXPENSES				BALANCE
DATE	TRANSACTION DETAILS	Expense Debit (-)	Income Credit (+)	

Sheet Number ________________

INCOME & EXPENSES				BALANCE
DATE	TRANSACTION DETAILS	Expense Debit (-)	Income Credit (+)	

Sheet Number ______________

INCOME & EXPENSES				BALANCE
DATE	TRANSACTION DETAILS	Expense Debit (-)	Income Credit (+)	

Sheet Number ________________

INCOME & EXPENSES				BALANCE
DATE	TRANSACTION DETAILS	Expense Debit (-)	Income Credit (+)	

Sheet Number ___________________

INCOME & EXPENSES				BALANCE
DATE	TRANSACTION DETAILS	Expense Debit (-)	Income Credit (+)	

Sheet Number ________________

INCOME & EXPENSES				BALANCE
DATE	TRANSACTION DETAILS	<u>Expense</u> Debit (-)	<u>Income</u> Credit (+)	

Sheet Number ________________

INCOME & EXPENSES				BALANCE
DATE	TRANSACTION DETAILS	Expense Debit (-)	Income Credit (+)	

Sheet Number ________________

INCOME & EXPENSES				BALANCE
DATE	TRANSACTION DETAILS	Expense Debit (-)	Income Credit (+)	

Sheet Number ________________

INCOME & EXPENSES				BALANCE
DATE	TRANSACTION DETAILS	Expense Debit (-)	Income Credit (+)	

Sheet Number ________________

INCOME & EXPENSES				BALANCE
DATE	TRANSACTION DETAILS	Expense Debit (-)	Income Credit (+)	

Sheet Number ________________

INCOME & EXPENSES				BALANCE
DATE	TRANSACTION DETAILS	Expense Debit (-)	Income Credit (+)	

Sheet Number ________________

INCOME & EXPENSES					BALANCE
DATE	TRANSACTION DETAILS	Expense Debit (-)	Income Credit (+)		

Sheet Number ________________

INCOME & EXPENSES				BALANCE
DATE	TRANSACTION DETAILS	Expense Debit (-)	Income Credit (+)	

Sheet Number _______________

INCOME & EXPENSES				BALANCE
DATE	TRANSACTION DETAILS	Expense Debit (-)	Income Credit (+)	

Sheet Number ________________

INCOME & EXPENSES				BALANCE
DATE	TRANSACTION DETAILS	Expense Debit (-)	Income Credit (+)	

Sheet Number ________________

INCOME & EXPENSES				BALANCE
DATE	TRANSACTION DETAILS	Expense Debit (-)	Income Credit (+)	

Sheet Number ________________

INCOME & EXPENSES				BALANCE
DATE	TRANSACTION DETAILS	Expense Debit (-)	Income Credit (+)	

Sheet Number ________________

INCOME & EXPENSES				BALANCE
DATE	TRANSACTION DETAILS	Expense Debit (-)	Income Credit (+)	

Sheet Number ________________

INCOME & EXPENSES				BALANCE
DATE	TRANSACTION DETAILS	Expense Debit (-)	Income Credit (+)	

Sheet Number ________________

INCOME & EXPENSES				BALANCE
DATE	TRANSACTION DETAILS	Expense Debit (-)	Income Credit (+)	

Sheet Number ________________

INCOME & EXPENSES				BALANCE
DATE	TRANSACTION DETAILS	Expense Debit (-)	Income Credit (+)	

Sheet Number ________________

INCOME & EXPENSES				BALANCE
DATE	TRANSACTION DETAILS	Expense Debit (-)	Income Credit (+)	

Sheet Number ________________

INCOME & EXPENSES				BALANCE
DATE	TRANSACTION DETAILS	Expense Debit (-)	Income Credit (+)	

Sheet Number ________________

INCOME & EXPENSES				BALANCE
DATE	TRANSACTION DETAILS	Expense Debit (-)	Income Credit (+)	

Sheet Number ________________

INCOME & EXPENSES				BALANCE
DATE	TRANSACTION DETAILS	Expense Debit (-)	Income Credit (+)	

Sheet Number ________________

INCOME & EXPENSES				BALANCE
DATE	TRANSACTION DETAILS	Expense Debit (-)	Income Credit (+)	

Sheet Number ________________

INCOME & EXPENSES				BALANCE
DATE	TRANSACTION DETAILS	Expense Debit (-)	Income Credit (+)	

Sheet Number ________________

INCOME & EXPENSES				BALANCE
DATE	TRANSACTION DETAILS	Expense Debit (-)	Income Credit (+)	

Sheet Number ________________

INCOME & EXPENSES				BALANCE
DATE	TRANSACTION DETAILS	Expense Debit (-)	Income Credit (+)	

Sheet Number ________________

INCOME & EXPENSES				BALANCE
DATE	TRANSACTION DETAILS	Expense Debit (-)	Income Credit (+)	

Sheet Number ________________

INCOME & EXPENSES				BALANCE
DATE	TRANSACTION DETAILS	Expense Debit (-)	Income Credit (+)	

Sheet Number ________________

INCOME & EXPENSES				BALANCE
DATE	TRANSACTION DETAILS	Expense Debit (-)	Income Credit (+)	

Sheet Number ________________

INCOME & EXPENSES				BALANCE
DATE	TRANSACTION DETAILS	Expense Debit (-)	Income Credit (+)	

Sheet Number ________________

INCOME & EXPENSES				BALANCE
DATE	TRANSACTION DETAILS	Expense Debit (-)	Income Credit (+)	

Sheet Number ________________

INCOME & EXPENSES				BALANCE
DATE	TRANSACTION DETAILS	Expense Debit (-)	Income Credit (+)	

Sheet Number ________________

INCOME & EXPENSES				BALANCE
DATE	TRANSACTION DETAILS	Expense Debit (-)	Income Credit (+)	

Sheet Number ________________

INCOME & EXPENSES				BALANCE
DATE	TRANSACTION DETAILS	Expense Debit (-)	Income Credit (+)	

Sheet Number ___________________

INCOME & EXPENSES				BALANCE
DATE	TRANSACTION DETAILS	Expense Debit (-)	Income Credit (+)	

Sheet Number ________________

INCOME & EXPENSES				BALANCE
DATE	TRANSACTION DETAILS	Expense Debit (-)	Income Credit (+)	

Sheet Number ________________

INCOME & EXPENSES				BALANCE
DATE	TRANSACTION DETAILS	Expense Debit (-)	Income Credit (+)	

Sheet Number ________________

INCOME & EXPENSES				BALANCE
DATE	TRANSACTION DETAILS	Expense Debit (-)	Income Credit (+)	

Sheet Number ________________

INCOME & EXPENSES				BALANCE
DATE	TRANSACTION DETAILS	Expense Debit (-)	Income Credit (+)	

Sheet Number ________________

INCOME & EXPENSES				BALANCE
DATE	TRANSACTION DETAILS	Expense Debit (-)	Income Credit (+)	

Sheet Number ________________

INCOME & EXPENSES				BALANCE
DATE	TRANSACTION DETAILS	<u>Expense</u> Debit (-)	<u>Income</u> Credit (+)	

Sheet Number ____________

INCOME & EXPENSES				BALANCE
DATE	TRANSACTION DETAILS	Expense Debit (-)	Income Credit (+)	

Sheet Number ________________

INCOME & EXPENSES				BALANCE
DATE	TRANSACTION DETAILS	Expense Debit (-)	Income Credit (+)	

Sheet Number ________________

INCOME & EXPENSES				BALANCE
DATE	TRANSACTION DETAILS	Expense Debit (-)	Income Credit (+)	

Sheet Number ________________

INCOME & EXPENSES				BALANCE
DATE	TRANSACTION DETAILS	Expense Debit (-)	Income Credit (+)	

Sheet Number ____________________

INCOME & EXPENSES				BALANCE
DATE	TRANSACTION DETAILS	Expense Debit (-)	Income Credit (+)	

Sheet Number ________________

INCOME & EXPENSES				BALANCE
DATE	TRANSACTION DETAILS	Expense Debit (-)	Income Credit (+)	

Sheet Number ________________

INCOME & EXPENSES				BALANCE
DATE	TRANSACTION DETAILS	Expense Debit (-)	Income Credit (+)	

Sheet Number ________________

INCOME & EXPENSES				BALANCE
DATE	TRANSACTION DETAILS	Expense Debit (-)	Income Credit (+)	

Sheet Number ________________

INCOME & EXPENSES				BALANCE
DATE	TRANSACTION DETAILS	Expense Debit (-)	Income Credit (+)	

Sheet Number ________________

INCOME & EXPENSES				BALANCE
DATE	TRANSACTION DETAILS	Expense Debit (-)	Income Credit (+)	

Sheet Number _______________

INCOME & EXPENSES				BALANCE
DATE	TRANSACTION DETAILS	Expense Debit (-)	Income Credit (+)	

Sheet Number ________________

INCOME & EXPENSES				BALANCE
DATE	TRANSACTION DETAILS	<u>Expense</u> Debit (-)	<u>Income</u> Credit (+)	

Sheet Number ________________

INCOME & EXPENSES				BALANCE
DATE	TRANSACTION DETAILS	Expense Debit (-)	Income Credit (+)	

Sheet Number ________________

INCOME & EXPENSES				BALANCE
DATE	TRANSACTION DETAILS	Expense Debit (-)	Income Credit (+)	

Sheet Number ___________________

INCOME & EXPENSES				BALANCE
DATE	TRANSACTION DETAILS	Expense Debit (-)	Income Credit (+)	

Sheet Number ________________

INCOME & EXPENSES				BALANCE
DATE	TRANSACTION DETAILS	Expense Debit (-)	Income Credit (+)	

Sheet Number ________________

INCOME & EXPENSES				BALANCE
DATE	TRANSACTION DETAILS	Expense Debit (-)	Income Credit (+)	

Sheet Number ________________

INCOME & EXPENSES				BALANCE
DATE	TRANSACTION DETAILS	Expense Debit (-)	Income Credit (+)	

Sheet Number ________________

INCOME & EXPENSES				BALANCE
DATE	TRANSACTION DETAILS	Expense Debit (-)	Income Credit (+)	

Sheet Number ________________

INCOME & EXPENSES				BALANCE
DATE	TRANSACTION DETAILS	Expense Debit (-)	Income Credit (+)	

Sheet Number ________________

INCOME & EXPENSES				BALANCE
DATE	TRANSACTION DETAILS	Expense Debit (-)	Income Credit (+)	

Sheet Number ___________________

INCOME & EXPENSES				BALANCE
DATE	TRANSACTION DETAILS	Expense Debit (-)	Income Credit (+)	

Sheet Number ______________

INCOME & EXPENSES				BALANCE
DATE	TRANSACTION DETAILS	Expense Debit (-)	Income Credit (+)	

Sheet Number ________________

INCOME & EXPENSES				BALANCE
DATE	TRANSACTION DETAILS	Expense Debit (-)	Income Credit (+)	

BILL PLANNER

Date Range: ________

Payable to	Amount due		Due on	Notes	Paid (Y/N)

Notes

BILL PLANNER

Date Range: ________

Payable to	Amount due	Due on	Notes	Paid (Y/N)

Notes

BILL PLANNER

Date Range: ________

Payable to	Amount due		Due on	Notes	Paid (Y/N)

Notes

BILL PLANNER

Date Range: ________

Payable to	Amount due		Due on	Notes	Paid (Y/N)

Notes

BILL PLANNER

Date Range: ____________

Payable to	Amount due	Due on	Notes	Paid (Y/N)

Notes

BILL PLANNER **Date Range:** ________

Payable to	Amount due	Due on	Notes	Paid (Y/N)

Notes

BILL PLANNER

Date Range: ________

Payable to	Amount due		Due on	Notes	Paid (Y/N)

Notes

BILL PLANNER

Date Range: ________

Payable to	Amount due		Due on	Notes	Paid (Y/N)

Notes

BILL PLANNER

Date Range: ________

Payable to	Amount due		Due on	Notes	Paid (Y/N)

Notes

BILL PLANNER Date Range: ________

Payable to	Amount due	Due on	Notes	Paid (Y/N)

Notes

Made in the USA
Las Vegas, NV
16 November 2024

11958023R00070